MW00353736

**GRADES
2-3**

50 Skill-Building
Pyramid Puzzles:
MATH

Self-Checking Activity Pages That Motivate
Students to Practice Key Math Skills

IMMACULA A. RHODES

New York • Toronto • London • Auckland • Sydney
Mexico City • New Delhi • Hong Kong • Buenos Aires

Teaching *Resources*

In loving memory of Dad

"God has given us eternal life, and
this life is in his Son."
—1 JOHN 5:11

Cover design by Maria Lilja
Cover and interior illustrations by Teresa Anderko
Interior design by Kelli Thompson

ISBN: 978-0-545-27997-0

Text copyright © 2011 by Immacula A. Rhodes
Published by Scholastic Inc.

3 4 5 6 7 8 9 10   40   18 17 16 15 14 13 12

Contents

Contents

Introduction

The unique design of the activities in *50 Skill-Building Pyramid Puzzles: Math* gets students actively engaged in computing and practicing essential skills that help strengthen their math and problem-solving abilities. Each game-like puzzle challenges students to think about mathematical problems—the type of problems presented, the information provided, how to use that information, and the operations or methods needed to solve them. As they work their way up the pyramid, students fill in the answers to reveal a number code that can be used in solving the riddle at the top.

Much like the building blocks of a pyramid connect to one another, the problems that go up each side of these puzzles are mathematically connected. In order to move from one step to the next, students solve one problem at a time, starting at the bottom of the pyramid. After "climbing" both sides to the top, they use the numbers from the final problems to crack the code and answer the riddle. Math problems along the way require students to think about and use appropriate problem-solving strategies to arrive at the correct answer.

The problems are presented in a number of ways—equations, word problems, and graphics, to name a few—to give students a range of ways to view problems and consider strategies that might be used to solve them. Puzzles are grouped by topic and offer practice in a variety of skills including number patterns, place value, addition, subtraction, multiplication and division facts, time, money, measurement, and more.

The self-checking format of the puzzles allows you to use them in any number of ways. They work well for small-group or whole-class lessons, independent or partner activities, day starters, time-fillers, and even homework. Repeated practice in essential skills makes the puzzles ideal for reinforcing math concepts and challenging students to apply their understanding of math ideas to problem solving. In addition, the puzzles can be used as quick, informal assessments to help you monitor students' progress and math proficiency.

Once students solve a few of these intriguing puzzles, they'll be hooked. The activities can be completed in about 10 minutes and are fun, motivating, and chock full of opportunities to practice math skills. And best of all, students will be having such a good time, they won't even realize they're learning!

Connections to the Math Standards

The activities in this book are designed to support you in meeting national and state math standards. See page 7 for more.

Solving the Pyramid Puzzles

Students will enjoy solving the pyramid puzzles on their own. But, before they begin working independently, demonstrate how to solve a few puzzles to ensure they understand the steps and will succeed. As you work on the puzzles with students, you might use a think-aloud method to model strategies for solving the problems to complete the puzzles.

1. To begin, students solve the bottom problem on one side of the pyramid. They will use this answer to fill in the next box. They then look at the problem and/or directions on the next step and find the answer that goes there, and so on. As students work, encourage them to mentally ask questions such as: *What type of problem is this? What information is provided? How should that information be used? What methods or operations are needed to solve the problems?*

2. Students work their way up the pyramid in this manner, one problem at a time, until they've solved the last problem on that side. (Encourage them to recheck their answer to each problem before moving on to the next step.)

3. Once they complete one side of the pyramid, they solve the problems on the other side.

4. To crack the code for the riddle, students take the numbers from the final answer on each side of the pyramid and write them under the boxes at the top. Then they use the numbers and letters in the key to decode the answer to the riddle. For example, in the puzzle below, students write 1, 8, 2, 2, 1, 9 on the lines under the boxes. They check the key to find the letter corresponding to each number and write that letter in the box above the number. When finished, the answer to the riddle is revealed!

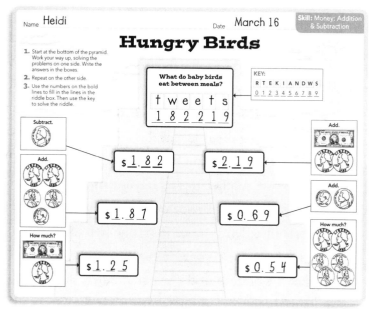

Tips for Working With the Puzzles

Try these quick and easy suggestions for using the puzzles and extending learning:

✲ Decide ahead of time whether you want to do the pyramid puzzles with the class as a whole, or have students work alone, in pairs, or in groups. Then choose a puzzle and make a copy for each student. For whole-class or small-group lessons, you might use an overhead projector or interactive whiteboard.

✲ At first, you might read and review how to solve each problem with students, especially beginners. Provide the necessary guidance to give students help with any problems they find difficult.

✲ For extra support, list the "answers" for the puzzles in random order on the board or chart paper. Have students solve the problems and check for their answers on the list before recording their responses on the puzzle.

The answer key for the math pyramid puzzles can be found on pages 61–64.

✱ If students get stuck on a particular step, you might ask them to talk through their problem-solving process to see if they can get themselves "unstuck." Offer students guidance where necessary, to help move them to the correct answer.

✱ After students complete the problems on the pyramid, encourage them to go back and check their answers before they fill in the numbers and letters to the riddle.

✱ Ask students to pair up and compare their answers after completing a puzzle. Encourage them to share their problem-solving strategy for each problem. Through sharing and discussion, students learn that more than one method might be used to solve the same problem. This also gives them the opportunity to communicate and evaluate their own thinking and processes when solving problems.

✱ Challenge students to solve the pyramids on pages 13–24 in reverse. To do this, fill in the answers on the left and right sides of a puzzle, leaving both bottom answers blank. Then mask all of the problems except those at the bottom on the left and right sides. Copy the puzzle and distribute it to students. To complete the puzzle, have students work from top to bottom, using the opposite operation to discover the missing problems and then writing them in the blank boxes. For example, if subtraction was used to solve the original puzzle, then students will use addition to come up with the missing problems. This activity helps students understand the inverse relationships of addition and subtraction.

✱ Use copies of pages 59 and 60, to make customized pyramid puzzles. (Mask the boxes in the riddle answer that aren't needed.) Or challenge students to make up their own math pyramid puzzles for classmates to solve.

Connections to the Math Standards

The activities in this book are designed to support you in meeting the following process standards for students in grades 2–3 recommended by the National Council of Teachers of Mathematics (NCTM):

Problem Solving: Apply mathematical skills confidently and meaningfully to unfamiliar situations. This is the overarching goal of math instruction.

Reasoning: Analyze, draw conclusions, and justify one's thinking. Gaining proficiency in these skills helps students develop a sense of self-reliance and confidence in their mathematical abilities and helps them see how thinking mathematically makes sense.

Communication: Use tools, such as reading, writing, modeling, drawing, and discussing to explore, convey, and clarify mathematical concepts and ideas.

Mathematical Connections: Notice how concepts and ideas in one area of math relate to other areas of math, other subject areas, and one's everyday life. Gaining awareness of mathematical connections fosters an appreciation of the usefulness of mathematics.

Representation: Create and use representations to organize, record, and communicate mathematical ideas. Students must acquire the ability to select, apply, and translate among mathematical representations to solve many different types of math problems.

Common Core State Standards

The activities in this book also correlate with the mathematics standards recommended by the Common Core State Standards Initiative, a state-led effort to establish a single set of clear educational standards whose aim is to provide students with high-quality education. At the time this book went to press, these standards were still being finalized. To learn more, go to www.corestandards.org.

> The grids on page 8 show how the activities correlate to the content standards for grades 2–3.

Connections to the NCTM Standards

Activity Title	Number & Operations	Algebra	Geometry	Measurement	Data Analysis & Probability
Place Value & Number Patterns					
Friendly Meeting	●				
Penny Pincher	●				
Treats-to-Glow	●	●			
Fin Flicks	●	●			
Addition					
Feline Fibber	●				
A Nosy Problem	●				
An Ill Sill	●				
The Chase Is On	●				
A Bad Day	●				
Sunny Times	●				
Subtraction					
Listen Up!	●				
A Gator's Game	●				
Bird Builder	●				
Enough to Eat	●				
Furry Groomer	●				
Hoppin' to the Music	●				
Multiplication					
Cat Carrier	●				
Pie Picking	●				
Frog Misfortune	●				
Tree of Fortune	●				
Warm Farewell	●				
Parting the Sea	●				
Division					
Warm Puppy	●				
Dressed for Work	●				
Just a Phase	●				
Sea Sick	●				

Activity Title	Number & Operations	Algebra	Geometry	Measurement	Data Analysis & Probability
Mixed Operations					
Awesome Agents	●				
Up and Down	●				
Nothing to Do	●				
Spooky Space	●				
Keeping in Touch	●				
Winded Birdie	●				
Fractions					
Baseball's Best	●				
Bee Pleaser	●				
Wandering Penguin	●				
From Here to There	●				
Time					
On the Road	●			●	
The Magic Word	●			●	
Cold Chills	●			●	
Simple Solution	●			●	
Money					
Hungry Birds	●			●	
Done With Dessert	●			●	
Kitty Lit	●			●	
In a Jam	●			●	
Measurement					
Day to Day	●			●	
Treat of the Week	●			●	
Through the Door	●			●	
Buzzing Around	●			●	
Too Many Legs	●			●	
Drink-It!	●			●	

Name _____

Date _____

Friendly Meeting

1. Start at the bottom of the pyramid. Work your way up, solving the problems on one side. Write the answers in the boxes.

2. Repeat on the other side.

3. Use the numbers on the bold lines to fill in the lines in the riddle box. Then use the key to solve the riddle.

KEY:

M	V	P	A	S	E	W	F	G	L
0	1	2	3	4	5	6	7	8	9

What does the sea do when it meets the beach?

It _____ _____ _____ _____ _____ .

Add:
5 tens 4 ones

Add:
9 tens 2 ones

Subtract:
4 tens 1 one

Write the number:
4 tens 9 ones

Subtract:
2 tens 5 ones

Add:
5 tens 1 one

Change the ones place to 7.

Write the number:
3 tens 9 ones

Name _____

Date _____

Penny Pincher

1. Start at the bottom of the pyramid. Work your way up, solving the problems on one side. Write the answers in the boxes.

2. Repeat on the other side.

3. Use the numbers on the bold lines to fill in the lines in the riddle box. Then use the key to solve the riddle.

KEY:

D	P	S	N	F	C	O	T	E	I
0	1	2	3	4	5	6	7	8	9

How much did it cost the skunk to leave the zoo?

One ___ ___ ___ ___ ___

Subtract:
2 hundreds 0 tens 0 ones

Subtract:
3 tens 3 ones

Change the hundreds place to 2.

Write the number:
5 hundreds 7 tens 0 ones

Subtract:
2 tens 7 ones

Subtract:
1 hundred 0 tens 6 ones

Change the hundreds place to 3.

Write the number:
2 hundreds 9 tens 1 one

Name _____

Date _____

Treats-to-Glow

1. Start at the bottom of the pyramid. Work your way up, solving the problems on one side. Write the answers in the boxes.

2. Repeat on the other side.

3. Use the numbers on the bold lines to fill in the lines in the riddle box. Then use the key to solve the riddle.

KEY:

G	L	S	E	B	I	X	T	P	H
0	1	2	3	4	5	6	7	8	9

What kind of snacks do fireflies eat?

_____ _____ _____ _____ _____ snacks

Find the missing number, then add:
10, 25, 40, _____

Find the missing number, then subtract:
16, _____, 26, 31

Find the missing number, then add:
49, 39, _____, 19

Find the missing number.
13, 20, 27, _____

Find the missing number, then subtract:
2, _____, 14, 20

Find the missing number, then add:
89, 78, _____, 56

Find the missing number, then subtract:
19, 14, _____, 4

Find the missing number.
_____, 105, 110, 115

Name _____

Date _____

Fin Flicks

1. Start at the bottom of the pyramid. Work your way up, solving the problems on one side. Write the answers in the boxes.

2. Repeat on the other side.

3. Use the numbers on the bold lines to fill in the lines in the riddle box. Then use the key to solve the riddle.

KEY:

Y	T	I	E	K	Q	D	R	V	N
0	1	2	3	4	5	6	7	8	9

What kind of movies do fish go to?

The ____ ____ ____ ____ - ____ ____ movies

Find the missing number, then add:
259, 271, ____, 295

Find the missing number, then subtract:
19, ____, 35, 43

Find the missing number, then subtract:
245, 240, 235, ____

Find the missing number.
101, 202, ____, 404

Find the missing number, then add:
173, 164, ____, 146

Find the missing number, then add:
432, ____, 448, 456

Find the missing number, then subtract:
13, 26, 39, ____

Find the missing number.
99, 92, ____, 78

Name _____

Date _____

Feline Fibber

1. Start at the bottom of the pyramid. Work your way up, solving the problems on one side. Write the answers in the boxes.

2. Repeat on the other side.

3. Use the numbers on the bold lines to fill in the lines in the riddle box. Then use the key to solve the riddle.

KEY:

S	P	G	A	F	N	O	K	I	L
0	1	2	3	4	5	6	7	8	9

What animal never tells the truth?

A ____ ____ ____ ____

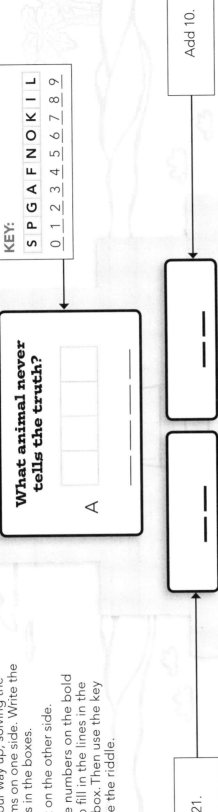

Add 10.

Add 11.

Add 21.

Add 12.

9 + 2 = ____

Add 21.

Add 9.

Add 30.

Add 15.

11 + 12 = ____

Name _____

Date _____

A Nosy Problem

1. Start at the bottom of the pyramid. Work your way up, solving the problems on one side. Write the answers in the boxes.

2. Repeat on the other side.

3. Use the numbers on the bold lines to fill in the lines in the riddle box. Then use the key to solve the riddle.

KEY:

X	P	T	I	H	V	E	O	C	F
0	1	2	3	4	5	6	7	8	9

What do you call a nose that's 12 inches long?

A _____ _____ _____ _____

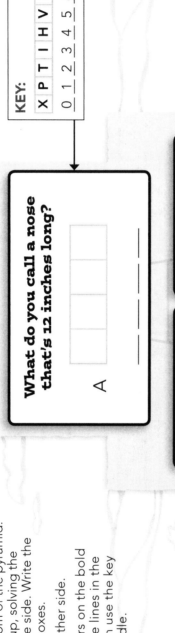

Add 14.

Add 8.

Add 17.

Add 20.

9 + 4 = _____

Add 41.

Add 15.

Add 22.

Add 9.

8 + 2 = _____

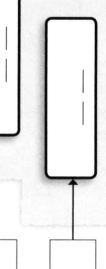

Name _____

Date _____

An Ill Sill

1. Start at the bottom of the pyramid. Work your way up, solving the problems on one side. Write the answers in the boxes.

2. Repeat on the other side.

3. Use the numbers on the bold lines to fill in the lines in the riddle box. Then use the key to solve the riddle.

KEY:

A	T	S	P	B	N	F	D	H	E
0	1	2	3	4	5	6	7	8	9

Why did the window go to the doctor?

It had ____ ____ ____ ____ ____ .

Add 7.

Add 15.

Add 10.

Add 15.

27 + 18 = ____ ____

Add 76.

Add 58.

Add 24.

Add 65.

49 + 33 = ____ ____

Name _____

Date _____

The Chase Is On

1. Start at the bottom of the pyramid. Work your way up, solving the problems on one side. Write the answers in the boxes.

2. Repeat on the other side.

3. Use the numbers on the bold lines in the lines in the riddle box. Then use the key to solve the riddle.

KEY:

T	C	S	H	B	K	R	A	J	E
0	1	2	3	4	5	6	7	8	9

What is harder to catch the faster you run?

Your ___ ___ ___ ___ ___

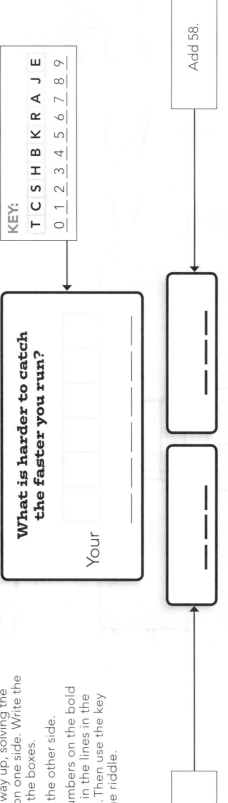

Add 58.

Add 63.

Add 29.

Add 17.

$501 + 35 = $ ___

Add 26.

Add 39.

Add 115.

Add 14.

$214 + 61 = $ ___

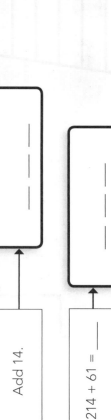

Name _____

Date _____

A Bad Day

1. Start at the bottom of the pyramid. Work your way up, solving the problems on one side. Write the answers in the boxes.

2. Repeat on the other side.

3. Use the numbers on the bold lines to fill in the lines in the riddle box. Then use the key to solve the riddle.

KEY:

V	E	K	Y	B	F	A	D	R	H
0	1	2	3	4	5	6	7	8	9

Which day of the week do chickens like the least?

_____ _____ _____ _____ - _____ _____ _____ :

Add 115.

Add 53.

Add 238.

Add 39.

$267 + 51 = $ _____

Add 37.

Add 129.

Add 76.

Add 204.

$98 + 39 = $ _____

Name _____

Date _____

Sunny Times

1. Start at the bottom of the pyramid. Work your way up, solving the problems on one side. Write the answers in the boxes.

2. Repeat on the other side.

3. Use the numbers on the bold lines to fill in the lines in the riddle box. Then use the key to solve the riddle.

KEY:

H	U	E	R	X	M	T	L	D	P
0	1	2	3	4	5	6	7	8	9

What do you call a snowman with a tan?

A _____

Add 266.

Add 100.

Add 127.

Add 104.

138 + 137 = _____

Add 121.

Add 157.

Add 249.

Add 112.

171 + 108 = _____

Name _____ Date _____

Listen Up!

1. Start at the bottom of the pyramid. Work your way up, solving the problems on one side. Write the answers in the boxes.

2. Repeat on the other side.

3. Use the numbers on the bold lines to fill in the lines in the riddle box. Then use the key to solve the riddle.

KEY:

N	O	C	R	U	L	B	V	I	F
0	1	2	3	4	5	6	7	8	9

What has ears but can't hear?

Subtract 10.

Subtract 13.

Subtract 12.

Subtract 3.

$79 - 11 =$ ___

Subtract 16.

Subtract 9.

Subtract 22.

Subtract 10.

$88 - 10 =$ ___

Name _____

Date _____

A Gator's Game

1. Start at the bottom of the pyramid. Work your way up, solving the problems on one side. Write the answers in the boxes.

2. Repeat on the other side.

3. Use the numbers on the bold lines to fill in the lines in the riddle box. Then use the key to solve the riddle.

KEY:

R	P	S	A	M	D	O	N	I	B
0	1	2	3	4	5	6	7	8	9

What is an alligator's favorite card game?

___ ___ ___ ___

Subtract 20.

Subtract 7.

Subtract 9.

Subtract 10.

89 – 12 = ___

Subtract 5.

Subtract 17.

Subtract 8.

Subtract 13.

99 – 29 = ___

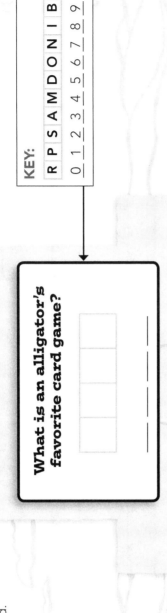

Name _____

Date _____

Bird Builder

1. Start at the bottom of the pyramid. Work your way up, solving the problems on one side. Write the answers in the boxes.
2. Repeat on the other side.
3. Use the numbers on the bold lines to fill in the lines in the riddle box. Then use the key to solve the riddle.

KEY:

R	W	A	C	Y	U	J	N	E	P
0	1	2	3	4	5	6	7	8	9

What bird is always welcome at a construction site?

A ___ ___ ___ ___ ___

Subtract 61.

Subtract 11.

Subtract 60.

Subtract 22.

$436 - 204 = $ ___

Subtract 40.

Subtract 63.

Subtract 105.

Subtract 151.

$694 - 33 = $ ___

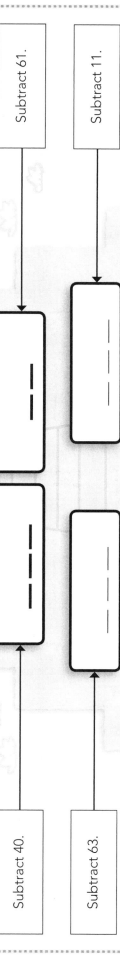

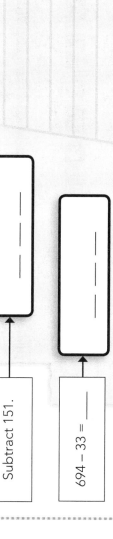

Name _____

Date _____

Enough to Eat

1. Start at the bottom of the pyramid. Work your way up, solving the problems on one side. Write the answers in the boxes.

2. Repeat on the other side.

3. Use the numbers on the bold lines to fill in the lines in the riddle box. Then use the key to solve the riddle.

KEY:

I	P	F	O	S	H	C	N	M	Z
0	1	2	3	4	5	6	7	8	9

How much food does a crab eat before it feels full?

Just a ___ ___ ___ ___ ___

Subtract 18.

Subtract 162.

Subtract 89.

Subtract 408.

$867 - 125 = $ ___

Subtract 106.

Subtract 49.

Subtract 66.

Subtract 135.

$572 - 109 = $ ___

Name _____

Date _____

Furry Groomer

1. Start at the bottom of the pyramid. Work your way up, solving the problems on one side. Write the answers in the boxes.

2. Repeat on the other side.

3. Use the numbers on the bold lines to fill in the lines in the riddle box. Then use the key to solve the riddle.

KEY:

T	F	H	J	E	L	P	N	O	Y
0	1	2	3	4	5	6	7	8	9

What kind of comb does a bear use?

A _____ _____ _____ _____ _____ comb

Subtract 132.

Subtract 89.

Subtract 25.

Subtract 163.

$669 - 211 =$ _____

Subtract 63.

Subtract 138.

Subtract 206.

Subtract 55.

$789 - 40 =$ _____

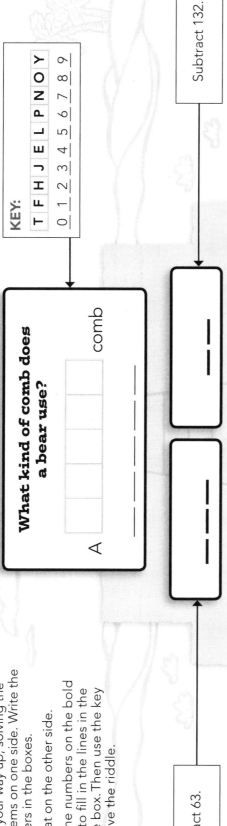

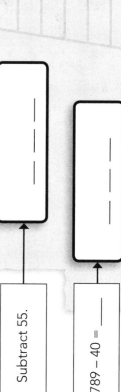

Name _____

Date _____

Hoppin' to the Music

1. Start at the bottom of the pyramid. Work your way up, solving the problems on one side. Write the answers in the boxes.

2. Repeat on the other side.

3. Use the numbers on the bold lines to fill in the lines in the riddle box. Then use the key to solve the riddle.

KEY:

X	H	O	Q	K	Z	R	P	I	M
0	1	2	3	4	5	6	7	8	9

What is a rabbit's favorite kind of music?

___ ___ ___ ___ - ___ ___ ___ ___ !

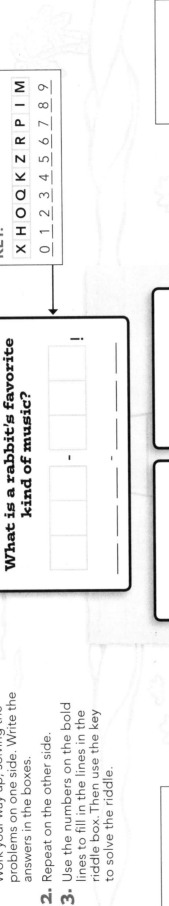

Subtract 149.

Subtract 345.

Subtract 74.

Subtract 114.

941 – 132 = ___

Subtract 108.

Subtract 233.

Subtract 68.

Subtract 162.

867 – 109 = ___ ___ ___

Name _____

Date _____

Cat Carrier

1. Start at the bottom of the pyramid. Work your way up, solving the problems on one side. Write the answers in the boxes.

2. Repeat on the other side.

3. Use the numbers on the bold lines to fill in the lines in the riddle box. Then use the key to solve the riddle.

KEY:

Q	A	U	L	P	R	H	G	W	T
0	1	2	3	4	5	6	7	8	9

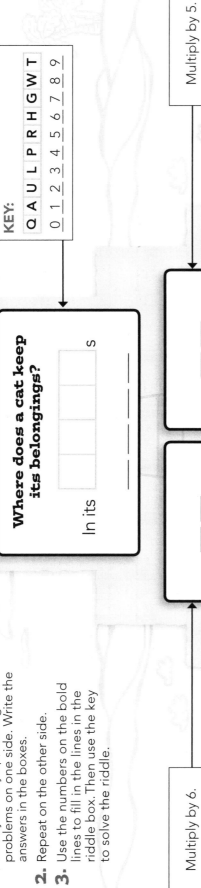

Where does a cat keep its belongings?

In its _____ ____ ____ ____ s

Multiply by 5.

Subtract 13.

Multiply by 4.

Subtract 8.

7 × 2 = _____

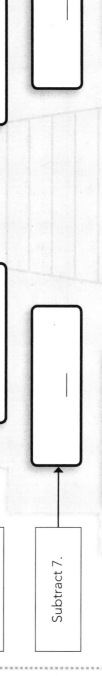

Multiply by 6.

Subtract 9.

Multiply by 2.

Subtract 7.

5 × 3 = _____

Name _____

Date _____

Pie Picking

1. Start at the bottom of the pyramid. Work your way up, solving the problems on one side. Write the answers in the boxes.

2. Repeat on the other side.

3. Use the numbers on the bold lines to fill in the lines in the riddle box. Then use the key to solve the riddle.

KEY:

L	H	K	P	O	F	I	R	T	A
0	1	2	3	4	5	6	7	8	9

What is the best thing to put in a pie?

A ____ ____ ____ ____ !

Multiply by 8.

Subtract 51.

Multiply by 5.

Multiply by 4.

$3 \times 1 = $ ____

Multiply by 9.

Subtract 50.

Multiply by 7.

Multiply by 2.

$2 \times 2 = $ ____

Name _____

Date _____

Frog Misfortune

1. Start at the bottom of the pyramid. Work your way up, solving the problems on one side. Write the answers in the boxes.

2. Repeat on the other side.

3. Use the numbers on the bold lines to fill in the lines in the riddle box. Then use the key to solve the riddle.

KEY:

L	B	O	A	W	D	M	T	E	R
0	1	2	3	4	5	6	7	8	9

What happened to the frog's car when it broke down?

It got ____ ____ ____ ____ .

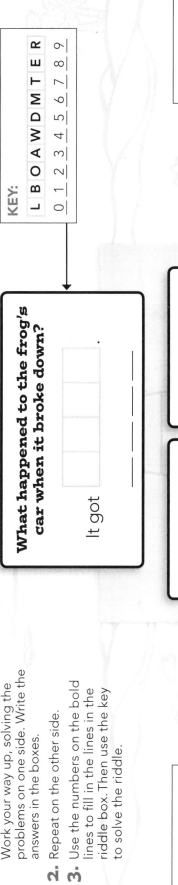

Multiply by 7.

Subtract 31.

Multiply by 9.

Subtract 44.

$8 \times 6 =$ ____

Multiply by 8.

Subtract 9.

Multiply by 6.

Subtract 60.

$9 \times 7 =$ ____

Name _____

Date _____

Tree of Fortune

1. Start at the bottom of the pyramid. Work your way up, solving the problems on one side. Write the answers in the boxes.

2. Repeat on the other side.

3. Use the numbers on the bold lines to fill in the lines in the riddle box. Then use the key to solve the riddle.

KEY:

Q	A	M	T	R	N	U	L	P	E
0	1	2	3	4	5	6	7	8	9

What is a fortune-teller's favorite tree?

A _____ _____ _____ _____ tree

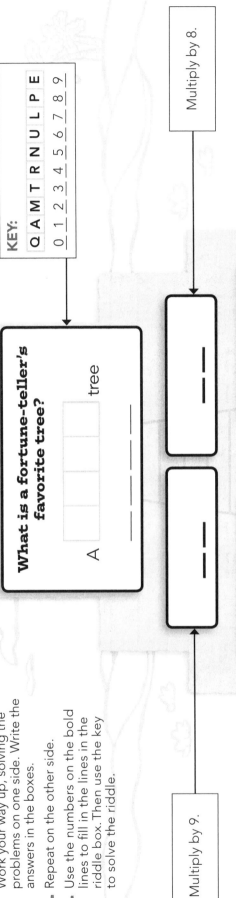

Multiply by 8.

Subtract 61.

Multiply by 7.

Subtract 11.

3 × 7 = _____

Multiply by 9.

Subtract 18.

Multiply by 9.

Subtract 33.

4 × 9 = _____

Name _____

Date _____

Warm Farewell

1. Start at the bottom of the pyramid. Work your way up, solving the problems on one side. Write the answers in the boxes.

2. Repeat on the other side.

3. Use the numbers on the bold lines to fill in the lines in the riddle box. Then use the key to solve the riddle.

KEY:

P	S	T	M	E	U	D	I	L	K
0	1	2	3	4	5	6	7	8	9

What did the banana do when the ice cream melted?

It ___ ___ ___ ___ ___ .

Multiply by 12.

Subtract 57.

Multiply by 9.

Subtract 5.

4 × 3 = ___

Multiply by 12.

Subtract 26.

Multiply by 5.

Subtract 47.

6 × 9 = ___

Name _____

Date _____

Parting the Sea

1. Start at the bottom of the pyramid. Work your way up, solving the problems on one side. Write the answers in the boxes.

2. Repeat on the other side.

3. Use the numbers on the bold lines to fill in the lines in the riddle box. Then use the key to solve the riddle.

KEY:

W	S	A	E	X	H	J	L	D	R
0	1	2	3	4	5	6	7	8	9

What do you use to cut an ocean in half?

A ___ ___ ___ ___   ___ ___

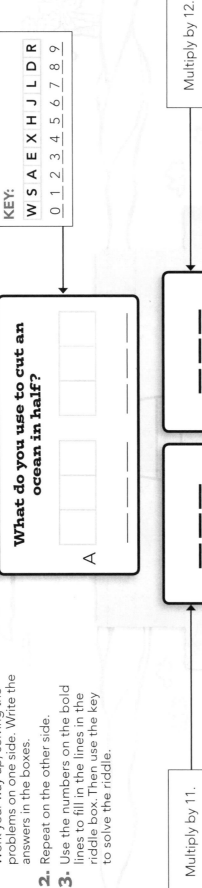

Multiply by 12.

Subtract 44.

Multiply by 9.

Subtract 10.

$2 \times 8 =$ ___

Multiply by 11.

Subtract 69.

Multiply by 9.

Subtract 21.

$5 \times 6 =$ ___

Name _____

Date _____

Warm Puppy

1. Start at the bottom of the pyramid. Work your way up, solving the problems on one side. Write the answers in the boxes.

2. Repeat on the other side.

3. Use the numbers on the bold lines to fill in the lines in the riddle box. Then use the key to solve the riddle.

KEY:

E	H	Z	L	S	O	R	P	T	N
0	1	2	3	4	5	6	7	8	9

What do you call a dog that always has a fever?

A [ ][ ][ ] _____ dog

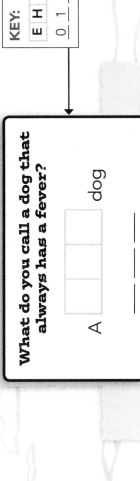

Divide by 2.

Add 9.

Divide by 6.

Add 30.

$36 \div 3 =$ _____

Add 9.

Divide by 5.

Add 25.

Divide by 2.

$40 \div 4 =$ _____

Name _____

Date _____

Dressed for Work

1. Start at the bottom of the pyramid. Work your way up, solving the problems on one side. Write the answers in the boxes.

2. Repeat on the other side.

3. Use the numbers on the bold lines to fill in the lines in the riddle box. Then use the key to solve the riddle.

KEY:

N	X	P	H	L	A	E	S	T	W
0	1	2	3	4	5	6	7	8	9

What did the lawyer wear to court?

A ___ ___ ___ ___ suit

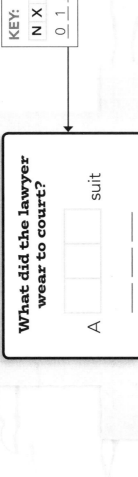

Divide by 3.

Add 25.

Divide by 8.

Add 10.

$54 \div 9 =$ ___

Add 33.

Divide by 5.

Add 56.

Divide by 2.

$56 \div 7 =$ ___

Name _____

Date _____

Just a Phase

1. Start at the bottom of the pyramid. Work your way up, solving the problems on one side. Write the answers in the boxes.

2. Repeat on the other side.

3. Use the numbers on the bold lines to fill in the lines in the riddle box. Then use the key to solve the riddle.

KEY:

U	L	D	R	G	B	E	F	T	J
0	1	2	3	4	5	6	7	8	9

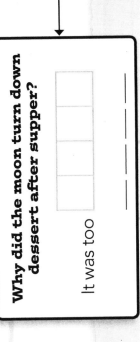

Why did the moon turn down dessert after supper?

It was too ____ ____ ____ ____

Divide by 4.

Add 40.

Divide by 7.

Add 20.

$72 \div 9 =$ ____

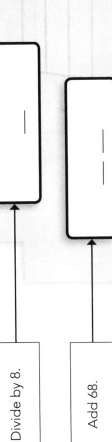

Add 61.

Divide by 8.

Add 68.

Divide by 2.

$48 \div 6 =$ ____

Name _____

Date _____

Sea Sick

1. Start at the bottom of the pyramid. Work your way up, solving the problems on one side. Write the answers in the boxes.

2. Repeat on the other side.

3. Use the numbers on the bold lines to fill in the lines in the riddle box. Then use the key to solve the riddle.

KEY:

K	C	S	E	D	B	H	L	Y	O
0	1	2	3	4	5	6	7	8	9

Where do sick boats go to get well?

To the __ __ __ __

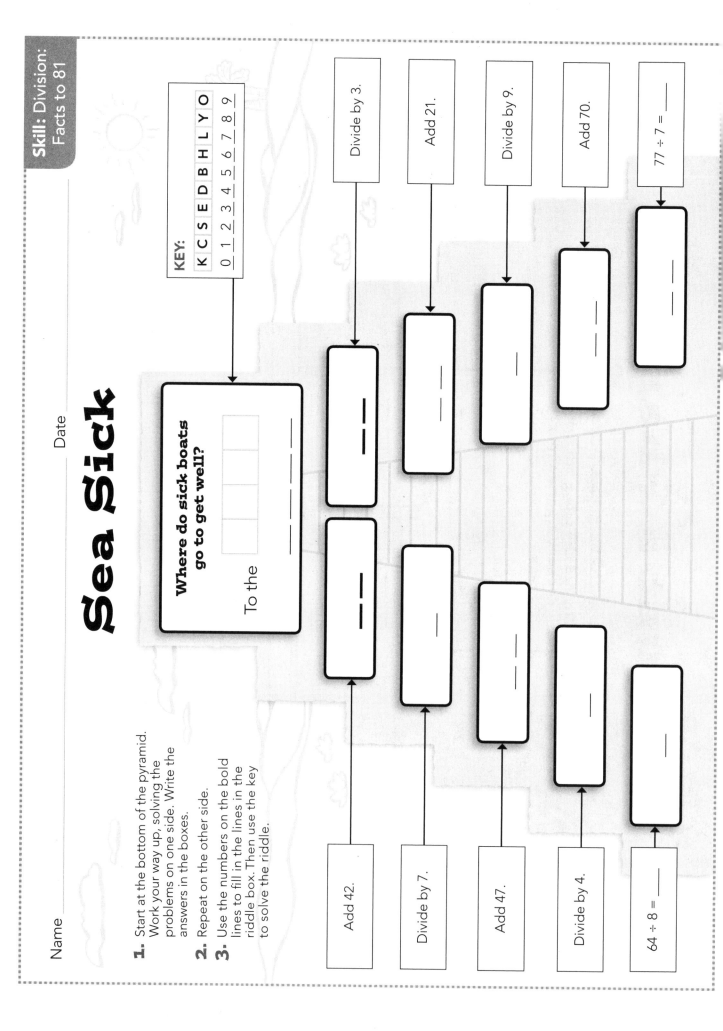

Divide by 3.

Add 21.

Divide by 9.

Add 70.

$77 \div 7 = $ ___

Add 42.

Divide by 7.

Add 47.

Divide by 4.

$64 \div 8 = $ ___

Awesome Agents

1. Start at the bottom of the pyramid. Work your way up, solving the problems on one side. Write the answers in the boxes.

2. Repeat on the other side.

3. Use the numbers on the bold lines to fill in the lines in the riddle box. Then use the key to solve the riddle.

KEY:

P	S	U	R	D	H	C	E	Y	N
0	1	2	3	4	5	6	7	8	9

What critter makes the best secret agent?

A ___ ___ ___ - ___ ___ ___

Add 400.

Change the tens place to 7.

Subtract 16.

Add 12.

$9 + 8 =$ ___

Subtract 10.

Add 101.

Change the ones place to 7.

Add 5.

$6 + 7 =$ ___

Name _____   Date _____

Up and Down

1. Start at the bottom of the pyramid. Work your way up, solving the problems on one side. Write the answers in the boxes.

2. Repeat on the other side.

3. Use the numbers on the bold lines to fill in the lines in the riddle box. Then use the key to solve the riddle.

What goes up and down but never moves?

KEY:

R	V	T	U	I	S	A	P	D	G
0	1	2	3	4	5	6	7	8	9

Subtract 371.

Add 54.

Subtract 61.

Change the tens place to 8.

$729 - 16 = $ _____

Change the hundreds place to 5.

Add 76.

Add 39.

Subtract 84.

$143 + 252 = $ _____

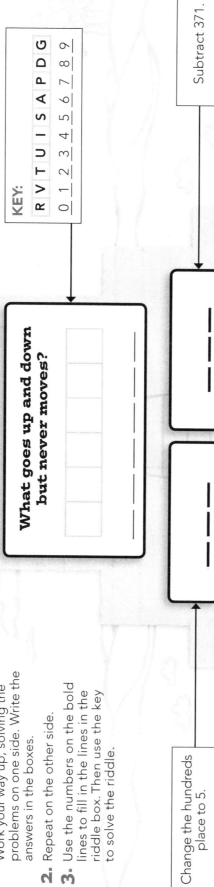

Name _____

Date _____

Nothing to Do

1. Start at the bottom of the pyramid. Work your way up, solving the problems on one side. Write the answers in the boxes.

2. Repeat on the other side.

3. Use the numbers on the bold lines to fill in the lines in the riddle box. Then use the key to solve the riddle.

KEY:

W	T	R	S	G	B	Y	D	O	E
0	1	2	3	4	5	6	7	8	9

What do you call a piece of wood that has nothing to do?

_____ _____ _____ _____ _____

Add 224.

Subtract 23.

Add 74.

Subtract 11.

97 – 64 = _____

Add 31.

Subtract 53.

Add 18.

Subtract 37.

63 + 36 = _____

Name _____

Date _____

Spooky Space

1. Start at the bottom of the pyramid. Work your way up, solving the problems on one side. Write the answers in the boxes.

2. Repeat on the other side.

3. Use the numbers on the bold lines to fill in the lines in the riddle box. Then use the key to solve the riddle.

KEY:

C	V	U	L	X	N	O	G	S	I
0	1	2	3	4	5	6	7	8	9

What room do ghosts always stay out of?

The ___ ___ ___ ___ ___ ___ room

Subtract 24.

Add 423.

Subtract 77.

Add 249.

295 + 91 = ___

Add 53.

Add 119.

Subtract 87.

Subtract 38.

246 + 98 = ___

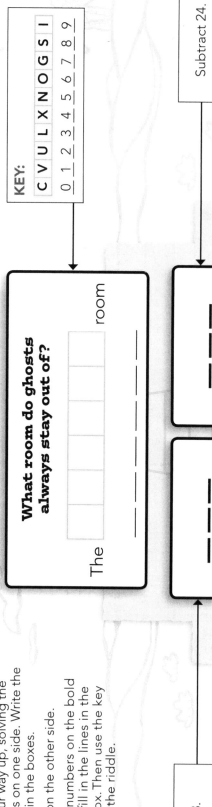
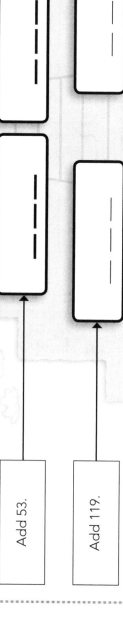
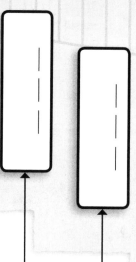

Keeping in Touch

1. Start at the bottom of the pyramid. Work your way up, solving the problems on one side. Write the answers in the boxes.

2. Repeat on the other side.

3. Use the numbers on the bold lines to fill in the lines in the riddle box. Then use the key to solve the riddle.

KEY:

O	L	A	N	P	R	I	G	H	S
0	1	2	3	4	5	6	7	8	9

What kind of pen pals can't read or write?

____ ____ ____ ____ !

Add 24.

Multiply by 11.

Divide by 5.

Add 4.

$3 \times 7 =$ ____

Add 16.

Multiply by 5.

Divide by 4.

Multiply by 2.

$4 \times 3 =$ ____

Name _____

Date _____

Winded Birdie

1. Start at the bottom of the pyramid. Work your way up, solving the problems on one side. Write the answers in the boxes.

2. Repeat on the other side.

3. Use the numbers on the bold lines to fill in the lines in the riddle box. Then use the key to solve the riddle.

KEY:

D	U	P	W	I	L	S	F	J	N
0	1	2	3	4	5	6	7	8	9

What kind of bird is always out of breath?

A ___ ___ ___ ___ ___ ___ ___

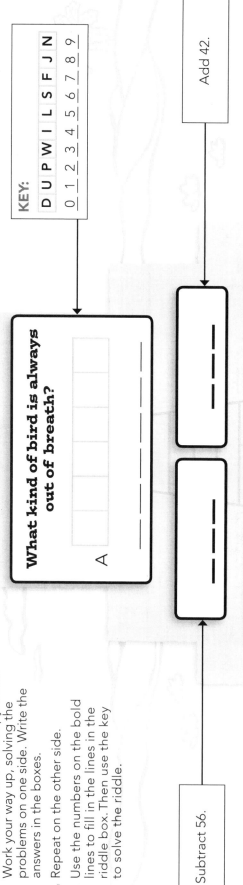

Subtract 56.

Subtract 42.

Add 264.

Subtract 21.

Divide by 6.

Add 628.

Add 27.

Multiply by 10.

$9 \times 3 = $ ___

$30 \div 3 = $ ___

Name _____   Date _____

Baseball's Best

1. Start at the bottom of the pyramid. Work your way up, solving the problems on one side. Write the answers in the boxes.

2. Repeat on the other side.

3. Use the numbers on the bold lines to fill in the lines in the riddle box. Then use the key to solve the riddle.

KEY:

S	B	N	Q	A	H	M	L	G	T
0	1	2	3	4	5	6	7	8	9

What animal is the best hitter in baseball?

A ___ ___ ___ ___

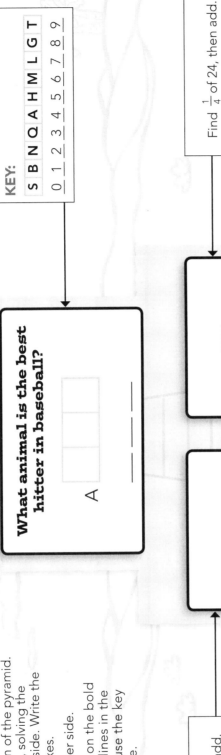

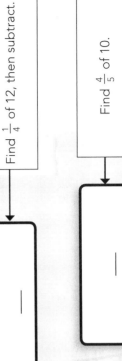

Find $\frac{1}{4}$ of 24, then add.

Find $\frac{1}{3}$ of 6, then subtract.

Find $\frac{1}{4}$ of 12, then subtract.

Find $\frac{4}{5}$ of 10.

Find $\frac{3}{4}$ of 16, then add.

Find $\frac{1}{2}$ of 14, then subtract.

Find $\frac{2}{3}$ of 9, then add.

Find $\frac{1}{2}$ of 6.

Name _____

Date _____

Bee Pleaser

1. Start at the bottom of the pyramid. Work your way up, solving the problems on one side. Write the answers in the boxes.

2. Repeat on the other side.

3. Use the numbers on the bold lines to fill in the lines in the riddle box. Then use the key to solve the riddle.

KEY:

X	M	A	Q	P	H	D	W	G	E
0	1	2	3	4	5	6	7	8	9

What is a bee's favorite kind of museum?

A _____ _____ museum

Carl gave away $\frac{1}{6}$ more of his cupcakes. How many does he have now?

Carl gave away $\frac{1}{3}$ more of his cupcakes. How many does he have now?

Carl baked 30 more cupcakes. How many does he have now?

Carl gave away $\frac{1}{2}$ of his 12 cupcakes. How many does he have now?

Kim gave away $\frac{2}{3}$ of her cookies. How many does she have now?

Kim bought 12 more cookies. How many does she have now?

Kim gave away $\frac{1}{2}$ more of her cookies. How many does she have now?

Kim gave away $\frac{1}{4}$ of her 24 cookies. How many does she have now?

Name _____

Date _____

Wandering Penguin

1. Start at the bottom of the pyramid. Work your way up, solving the problems on one side. Write the answers in the boxes.

2. Repeat on the other side.

3. Use the numbers on the bold lines to fill in the lines in the riddle box. Then use the key to solve the riddle.

KEY:

P	L	S	T	R	O	K	F	U	D
0	1	2	3	4	5	6	7	8	9

What do you call a penguin in the desert?

_____ _____ _____ _____ :

Sue bought 19 more pencils. How many does she have now?

Sue gave away $\frac{2}{3}$ more of her pencils. How many does she have now?

Sue gave away $\frac{1}{4}$ more of her pencils. How many does she have now?

Sue gave away $\frac{1}{2}$ of her 32 pencils. How many does she have now?

Dan gave away $\frac{1}{2}$ of his erasers. How many does he have now?

Dan's mom gave him 25 more erasers. How many does he have now?

Dan gave away $\frac{2}{3}$ more of his erasers. How many does he have now?

Dan gave away $\frac{1}{4}$ of his 20 erasers. How many does he have now?

Name _____

Date _____

From Here to There

1. Start at the bottom of the pyramid. Work your way up, solving the problems on one side. Write the answers in the boxes.

2. Repeat on the other side.

3. Use the numbers on the bold lines to fill in the lines in the riddle box. Then use the key to solve the riddle.

KEY:

R	O	D	U	J	E	C	K	G	P
0	1	2	3	4	5	6	7	8	9

What special object helps you walk through walls?

A ___ ___ ___ ___

Jan gave away $\frac{1}{2}$ more of her balloons. How many does she have now?

Jan gave away $\frac{1}{3}$ more of her balloons. How many does she have now?

Jan gave away $\frac{1}{6}$ more of her balloons. How many does she have now?

Jan gave away $\frac{1}{4}$ of her 48 balloons. How many does she have now?

Joe bought 11 more kites. How many does he have now?

Joe gave away $\frac{1}{2}$ more of his kites. How many does he have now?

Joe gave away $\frac{1}{5}$ more of his kites. How many does he have now?

Joe gave away $\frac{1}{6}$ of his 30 kites. How many does he have now?

Name _____

Date _____

On the Road

1. Start at the bottom of the pyramid. Work your way up, solving the problems on one side. Write the answers in the boxes.

2. Repeat on the other side.

3. Use the numbers on the bold lines to fill in the lines in the riddle box. Then use the key to solve the riddle.

KEY:

E	K	A	V	R	S	C	U	T	B
0	1	2	3	4	5	6	7	8	9

What does a glass car do when it comes to a stop sign?

It ____ ____ ____ ____ ____ ____ : ____ ____

What is the time 45 minutes later?

What is the time 15 minutes earlier?

What is the time?

What is the time 10 minutes earlier?

What is the time 20 minutes later?

What is the time?

Name _____

Date _____

The Magic Word

1. Start at the bottom of the pyramid. Work your way up, solving the problems on one side. Write the answers in the boxes.

2. Repeat on the other side.

3. Use the numbers on the bold lines to fill in the lines in the riddle box. Then use the key to solve the riddle.

KEY:

I	S	L	C	B	E	V	L	O	N
0	1	2	3	4	5	6	7	8	9

What can you break just by saying its name?

___ ___ ___ ___ ___ ___ ___

What is the time 45 minutes later?

__ : __

What is the time 15 minutes later?

__ : __

What is the time 20 minutes earlier?

__ : __

What is the time?

__ : __

What is the time 10 minutes earlier?

__ : __

What is the time 35 minutes later?

__ : __

What is the time 25 minutes later?

__ : __

What is the time?

__ : __

Name _____

Date _____

Cold Chills

1. Start at the bottom of the pyramid. Work your way up, solving the problems on one side. Write the answers in the boxes.

2. Repeat on the other side.

3. Use the numbers on the bold lines to fill in the lines in the riddle box. Then use the key to solve the riddle.

KEY:

R	S	C	A	I	T	E	L	P	N
0	1	2	3	4	5	6	7	8	9

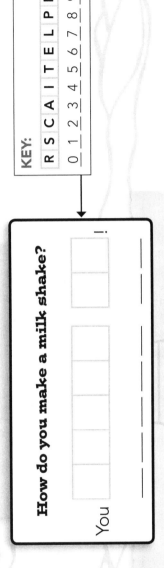

How do you make a milk shake?

You _____ _____ _____ _____ _____ ___ ___ ___ !

Supper is next and lasts 40 minutes. What time does it end?

Soccer practice is next and lasts 55 minutes. What time does it end?

The bus ride lasts 35 minutes. What time does it end?

What time does the bus leave school?

Lunch is next and lasts 45 minutes. What time does it end?

Reading is next and lasts 1 hour 40 minutes. What time does it end?

Morning Group lasts 50 minutes. What time does it end?

What time does Morning Group start?

Name _____

Date _____

Simple Solution

1. Start at the bottom of the pyramid. Work your way up, solving the problems on one side. Write the answers in the boxes.

2. Repeat on the other side.

3. Use the numbers on the bold lines to fill in the lines in the riddle box. Then use the key to solve the riddle.

KEY:

O	L	E	D	R	S	M	K	H	I
0	1	2	3	4	5	6	7	8	9

What can you put in a wooden box to make it weigh less?

_____ ____ ____ ____ ____

Subtract 10 minutes.

Add the minutes in $1\frac{1}{2}$ hour.

Add the minutes in a half hour.

How many minutes ____ 'til 2:00?

Subtract the minutes in a half hour.

Add the minutes in an hour.

Add the minutes in a quarter hour.

How many minutes have passed?

Name _____

Date _____

Hungry Birds

1. Start at the bottom of the pyramid. Work your way up, solving the problems on one side. Write the answers in the boxes.

2. Repeat on the other side.

3. Use the numbers on the bold lines to fill in the lines in the riddle box. Then use the key to solve the riddle.

KEY:

R	T	E	K	I	A	N	D	W	S
0	1	2	3	4	5	6	7	8	9

What do baby birds eat between meals?

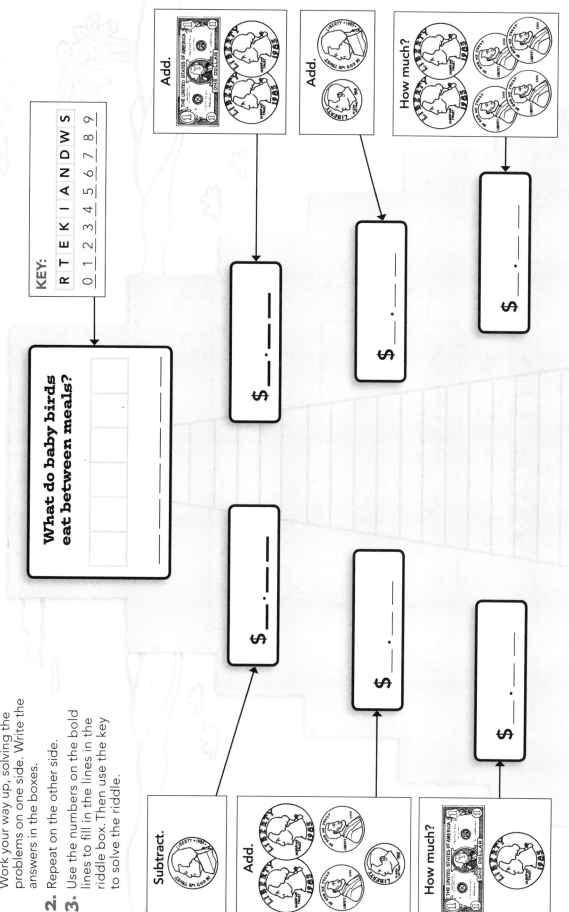

Add.

Add.

How much?

Subtract.

Add.

How much?

$ _ _ . _ _

$ _ _ . _ _

$ _ _ . _ _

$ _ _ . _ _

$ _ _ . _ _

$ _ _ . _ _

Name _____

Date _____

Done With Dessert

1. Start at the bottom of the pyramid. Work your way up, solving the problems on one side. Write the answers in the boxes.

2. Repeat on the other side.

3. Use the numbers on the bold lines to fill in the lines in the riddle box. Then use the key to solve the riddle.

How did the teddy bear feel after eating dessert?

___ ___ ___ ___ ___ ___ ___ !

KEY:

P	S	T	E	A	H	F	D	U	R
0	1	2	3	4	5	6	7	8	9

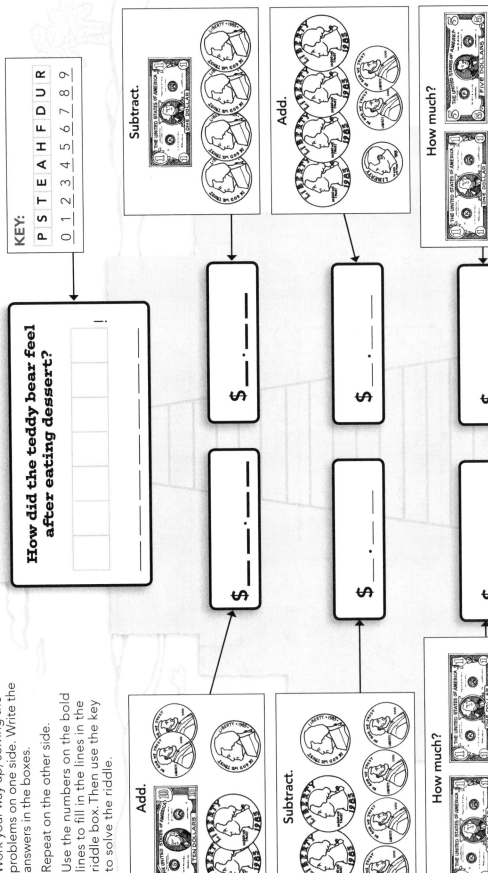

Subtract.

Add.

How much?

Add.

Subtract.

How much?

$ ___ ___ . ___ ___

$ ___ . ___ ___

$ ___ . ___ ___

$ ___ ___ . ___ ___

$ ___ . ___ ___

$ ___ . ___ ___

Name _____

Date _____

Kitty Lit

1. Start at the bottom of the pyramid. Work your way up, solving the problems on one side. Write the answers in the boxes.

2. Repeat on the other side.

3. Use the numbers on the bold lines to fill in the lines in the riddle box. Then use the key to solve the riddle.

KEY:

S	C	L	O	Q	A	T	R	H	G
0	1	2	3	4	5	6	7	8	9

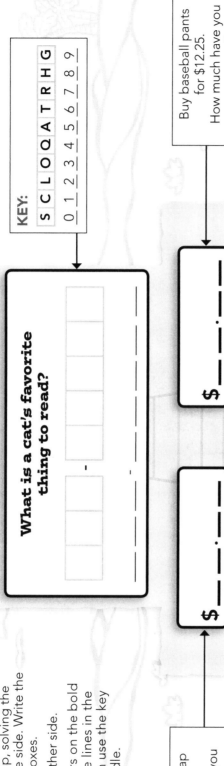

What is a cat's favorite thing to read?

Buy baseball pants for $12.25. How much have you spent in all?

$ ___ ___ . ___ ___

Buy a baseball shirt for $6.85. How much have you spent in all?

$ ___ ___ . ___ ___

One pair of socks cost $1.60. How much will you spend on 3 pairs of socks?

$ ___ ___ . ___ ___

Buy a baseball cap for $5.20. How much have you spent in all?

$ ___ ___ . ___ ___

Buy a bat for $6.95. How much have you spent in all?

$ ___ ___ . ___ ___

One baseball costs $1.75. How much will you spend on 2 baseballs?

$ ___ ___ . ___ ___

Name _____

Date _____

In a Jam

1. Start at the bottom of the pyramid. Work your way up, solving the problems on one side. Write the answers in the boxes.

2. Repeat on the other side.

3. Use the numbers on the bold lines to fill in the lines in the riddle box. Then use the key to solve the riddle.

KEY:

C	T	A	R	U	F	S	T	I	B
0	1	2	3	4	5	6	7	8	9

What kind of jam is not fit to eat?

A _ _ _ _ _ _ _ jam!

$ _ . _ _

$ _ . _ _

Buy sunglasses for $9.55.
How much do you have left?

$ _ . _ _

$ _ . _ _

Buy a hat for $7.15.
How much do you have left?

$ _ . _ _

$ _ . _ _

Buy a wristband for $3.10.
How much do you have left?

$ _ . _ _

$ _ . _ _

Start with $50.00 in your wallet.
Buy a pair of shoes for $24.40.
How much do you have left?

Buy a pack of pencils for $2.05.
How much do you have left?

Buy a bookbag for $15.80.
How much do you have left?

Buy a pack of paper for $1.65.
How much do you have left?

Start with $35.00 in your wallet.
Buy a notebook for $2.25.
How much do you have left?

Name _____

Date _____

Day to Day

1. Start at the bottom of the pyramid. Work your way up, solving the problems on one side. Write the answers in the boxes.

2. Repeat on the other side.

3. Use the numbers on the bold lines to fill in the lines in the riddle box. Then use the key to solve the riddle.

KEY:

D	W	B	I	K	P	N	E	X	C
0	1	2	3	4	5	6	7	8	9

What did the first Monday of the month say to the second Monday?

See you next

[ ] [ ] [ ] [ ] !

___ ___ ___ ___

Add the number of days in September.

___ ___

Add the number of days in 2 weeks.

___ ___

How many days are in April?

___ ___

Add the number of days in 1 week.

___ ___

Subtract the number of days in 3 weeks.

___ ___

How many days are in October?

___ ___

Name _____

Date _____

Treat of the Week

1. Start at the bottom of the pyramid. Work your way up, solving the problems on one side. Write the answers in the boxes.

2. Repeat on the other side.

3. Use the numbers on the bold lines to fill in the lines in the riddle box. Then use the key to solve the riddle.

KEY:

A	D	E	B	S	N	J	U	O	C
0	1	2	3	4	5	6	7	8	9

What is the yummiest day of the week?

☐ ☐ ☐ ☐ ☐ ☐ ☐

___ ___ ___ ___ ___ ___ ___

Add the number of days from August 17 to September 21.

Subtract the number of days in 7 weeks and 3 days.

Add the total number of days in April, May, and June.

How many days are in 4 weeks?

Subtract the number of days in 1 week minus 1 day.

Add the total number of days in October, November, and December.

Add the number of days from June 6 to June 30.

How many days are in 1 year?

Name _____

Date _____

Through the Door

1. Start at the bottom of the pyramid. Work your way up, solving the problems on one side. Write the answers in the boxes.

2. Repeat on the other side.

3. Use the numbers on the bold lines to fill in the lines in the riddle box. Then use the key to solve the riddle.

KEY:

J	Z	R	E	H	C	N	A	I	S
0	1	2	3	4	5	6	7	8	9

When is a door not a door?

When it is ___ ___ ___ ___ ___ !

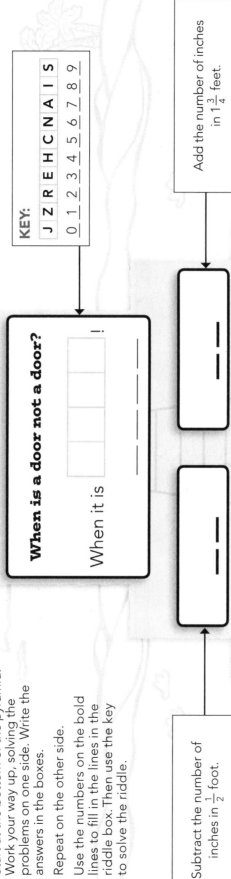

Add the number of inches in $1\frac{3}{4}$ feet.

Subtract the number of inches in $\frac{1}{4}$ foot.

Add the number of inches in 1 yard.

How many inches are in $1\frac{1}{2}$ feet?

Subtract the number of inches in $\frac{1}{2}$ foot.

Add the number of inches in 4 feet.

Add the number of inches in $\frac{1}{3}$ foot.

How many inches are in 2 feet?

Name _____

Date _____

Buzzing Around

1. Start at the bottom of the pyramid. Work your way up, solving the problems on one side. Write the answers in the boxes.

2. Repeat on the other side.

3. Use the numbers on the bold lines to fill in the lines in the riddle box. Then use the key to solve the riddle.

KEY:

D	W	O	Z	L	B	P	K	E	M
0	1	2	3	4	5	6	7	8	9

What do you call a bee that lives in a graveyard?

A ☐ ☐ ☐ - ☐ ☐ ☐ ☐

Travel back 59 miles. What milepost are you at?

Travel forward 275 miles more. What milepost are you at?

Travel forward 138 miles more. What milepost are you at?

Start at milepost 300, then travel back 66 miles. What milepost are you at?

Travel forward 132 miles. What milepost are you at?

Travel back 29 miles. What milepost are you at?

Travel forward 112 miles more. What milepost are you at?

Start at milepost 39, then travel forward 75 miles. What milepost are you at?

Too Many Legs

1. Start at the bottom of the pyramid. Work your way up, solving the problems on one side. Write the answers in the boxes.

2. Repeat on the other side.

3. Use the numbers on the bold lines to fill in the lines in the riddle box. Then use the key to solve the riddle.

50 Skill-Building Pyramid Puzzles: Math, Grades 2–3 © 2011 by Immacula A. Rhodes, Scholastic Teaching Resources • page 57

KEY:

F	V	I	E	K	S	D	W	B	A
0	1	2	3	4	5	6	7	8	9

What has four legs but only one foot?

___ ___ ___
A ___

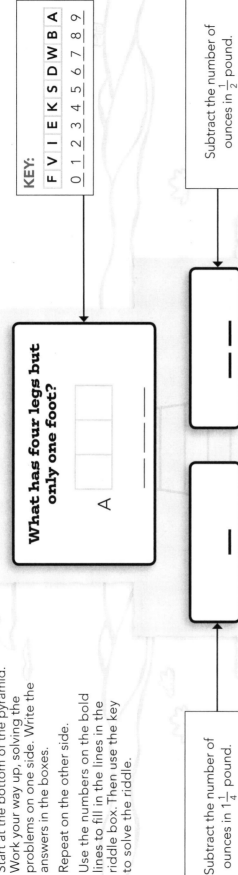

Subtract the number of ounces in $\frac{1}{2}$ pound.

Add the number of ounces in 2 pounds.

Subtract the number of ounces in $\frac{1}{4}$ pound.

How many ounces are in 1 pound?

Subtract the number of ounces in $1\frac{1}{4}$ pound.

Subtract the number of ounces in $\frac{1}{2}$ pound.

Subtract the number of ounces in $\frac{3}{4}$ pound.

How many ounces are in 3 pounds?

Name _____

Date _____

Drink-It!

1. Start at the bottom of the pyramid. Work your way up, solving the problems on one side. Write the answers in the boxes.

2. Repeat on the other side.

3. Use the numbers on the bold lines to fill in the lines in the riddle box. Then use the key to solve the riddle.

KEY:

R	T	O	A	C	P	K	F	M	U
0	1	2	3	4	5	6	7	8	9

What is a frog's favorite soft drink?

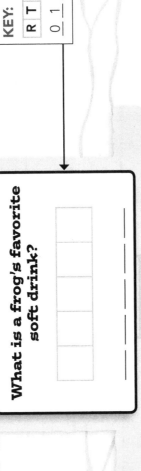

Subtract the number of ounces in 5 cups.

Add the number of ounces in 2 gallons.

Subtract the number of ounces in $1\frac{1}{2}$ cups.

How many ounces are in 1 quart?

Subtract the number of ounces in $\frac{1}{2}$ gallon.

Add the number of ounces in 1 cup.

Subtract the number of ounces in 2 pints.

How many ounces are in 1 gallon?

Name _____

Title _____

Date _____

1. Start at the bottom of the pyramid. Work your way up, solving the problems on one side. Write the answers in the boxes.

2. Repeat on the other side.

3. Use the numbers on the bold lines to fill in the lines in the riddle box. Then use the key to solve the riddle.

KEY:

0	1	2	3	4	5	6	7	8	9

Riddle:

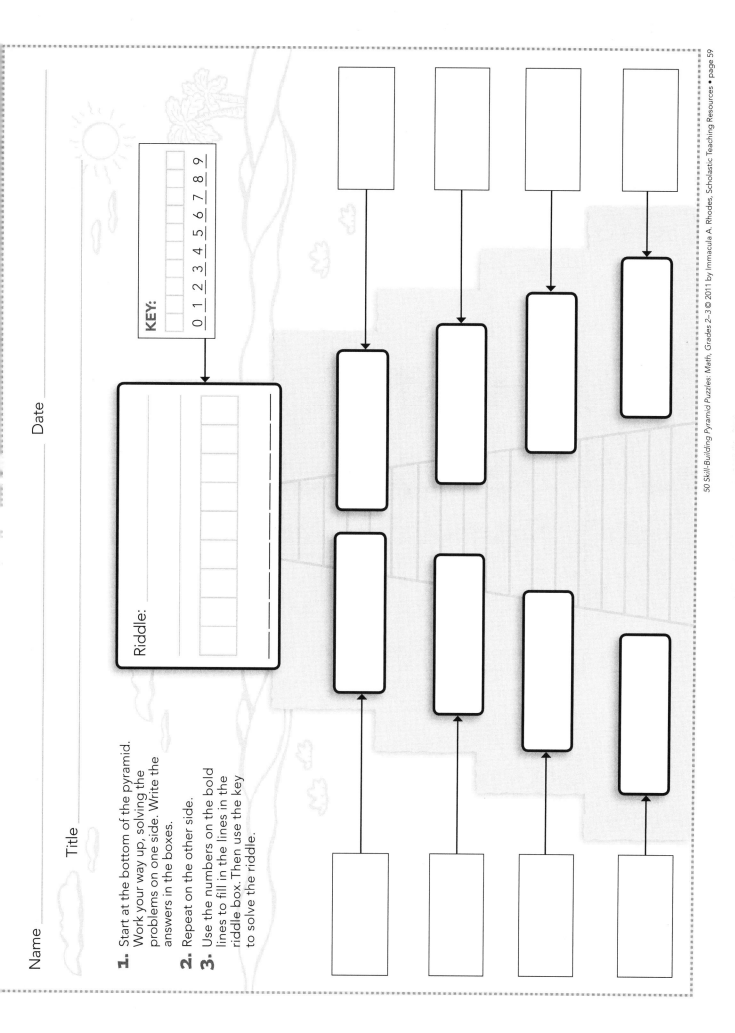

Name _____

Title _____

Date _____

1. Start at the bottom of the pyramid. Work your way up, solving the problems on one side. Write the answers in the boxes.

2. Repeat on the other side.

3. Use the numbers on the bold lines to fill in the lines in the riddle box. Then use the key to solve the riddle.

Riddle: _____

KEY:

0	1	2	3	4	5	6	7	8	9

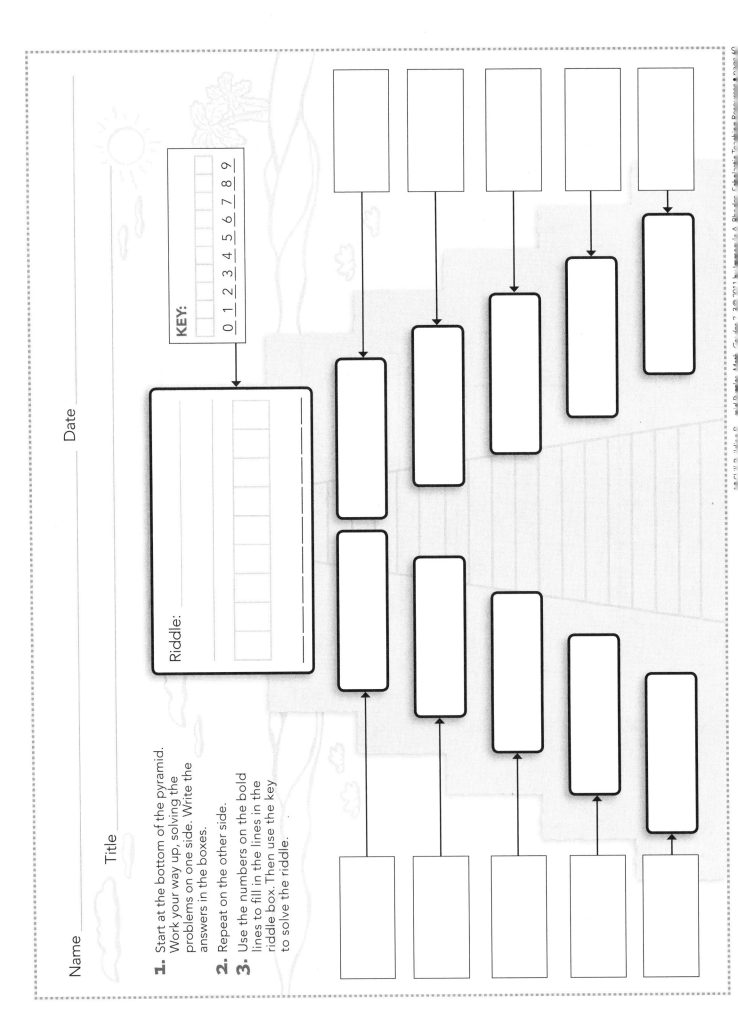

Answer Key

Page 9, **Friendly Meeting**
Riddle: waves
6,3,1,5,4

63	154
88	100
37	8
39	49

Page 13, **Feline Fibber**
Riddle: lion
9,8,6,5

98	65
77	55
68	44
38	23
23	11

Page 17, **A Bad Day**
Riddle: Fry-day
5,8,3-7,6,3

583	763
546	648
417	595
341	357
137	318

Page 10, **Penny Pincher**
Riddle: scent
2,5,8,3,7

258	37
285	237
391	270
291	570

Page 14, **A Nosy Problem**
Riddle: foot
9,7,7,2

97	72
56	58
41	50
19	33
10	13

Page 18, **Sunny Times**
Riddle: puddle
9,1,8,8,7,2

918	872
797	606
640	506
391	379
279	275

Page 11, **Treats-to-Glow**
Riddle: light
1,5,0,9,7

150	97
158	42
91	63
100	34

Page 15, **An Ill Sill**
Riddle: panes
3,0,5,9,2

305	92
229	85
171	70
147	60
82	45

Page 19, **Listen Up!**
Riddle: corn
2,1,3,0

21	30
37	40
46	53
68	65
78	68

Page 12, **Fin Flicks**
Riddle: dive-in
6,2,8,3-2,9

628	329
473	46
33	73
85	303

Page 16, **The Chase Is On**
Riddle: breath
4,6,9,7,0,3

469	703
443	645
404	582
289	553
275	536

Page 20, **A Gator's Game**
Riddle: snap
2,7,3,1

27	31
32	51
49	58
57	67
70	77

Page 21, **Bird Builder**
Riddle: crane
3,0,2,7,8

302	78
342	139
405	150
510	210
661	232

Page 25, **Cat Carrier**
Riddle: purr
4,2,5,5

42	55
7	11
16	24
8	6
15	14

Page 29, **Warm Farewell**
Riddle: split
1,0,8,7,2

108	72
9	6
35	63
7	7
54	12

Page 22, **Enough to Eat**
Riddle: pinch
1,0,7,6,5

107	65
213	83
262	245
328	334
463	742

Page 26, **Pie Picking**
Riddle: fork
5,4,7,2

54	72
6	9
56	60
8	12
4	3

Page 30, **Parting the Sea**
Riddle: sea saw
1,3,2   1,2,0

132	120
12	10
81	54
9	6
30	16

Page 23, **Furry Groomer**
Riddle: honey
2,8,7,4,9

287	49
350	181
488	270
694	295
749	458

Page 27, **Frog Misfortune**
Riddle: toad
7,2,3,5

72	35
9	5
18	36
3	4
63	48

Page 31, **Warm Puppy**
Riddle: hot
1,5,8

15	8
6	16
30	7
5	42
10	12

Page 24, **Hoppin' to the Music**
Riddle: hip-hop
1,8,7-1,2,7

187	127
295	276
528	621
596	695
758	809

Page 28, **Tree of Fortune**
Riddle: palm
8,1,7,2

81	72
9	9
27	70
3	10
36	21

Page 32, **Dressed for Work**
Riddle: law
4,5,9

45	9
12	27
60	2
4	16
8	6

Page 33, **Just a Phase**
Riddle: full
7,0,1,1

70	11
9	44
72	4
4	28
8	8

Page 37, **Nothing to Do**
Riddle: bored
5,8,2,9,7

58	297
27	73
80	96
62	22
99	33

Page 41, **Baseball's Best**
Riddle: bat
1,4,9

14	9
2	3
9	5
3	8

Page 34, **Sea Sick**
Riddle: dock
4,9,1,0

49	10
7	30
49	9
2	81
8	11

Page 38, **Spooky Space**
Riddle: living
3,9,1,9,5,7

391	957
338	981
219	558
306	635
344	386

Page 42, **Bee Pleaser**
Riddle: wax
7,2,0

7	20
21	24
9	36
18	6

Page 35, **Awesome Agents**
Riddle: spy-der
1,0,8-4,7,3

108	473
118	73
17	13
18	29
13	17

Page 39, **Keeping in Touch**
Riddle: pigs
4,6,7,9

46	79
30	55
6	5
24	25
12	21

Page 43, **Wandering Penguin**
Riddle: lost
1,5,2,3

15	23
30	4
5	12
15	16

Page 36, **Up and Down**
Riddle: stairs
5,2,6,4,0,5

526	405
426	776
350	722
311	783
395	713

Page 40, **Winded Birdie**
Riddle: puffin
2,1,7,7,4,9

217	749
273	707
9	728
54	100
27	10

Page 44, **From Here to There**
Riddle: door
2,1,1,0

21	10
10	20
20	30
25	36

Page 45, **On the Road**
Riddle: breaks
9,4,0,2,1,5

9:40	2:15
9:50	1:30
9:30	1:45

Page 50, **Done With Dessert**
Riddle: stuffed
1,2,8,6,6,3,7

$12.86	$6.37
$2.29	$7.57
$2.88	$6.45

Page 55, **Through the Door**
Riddle: ajar
7,0,7,2

70	72
76	51
28	54
24	18

Page 46, **The Magic Word**
Riddle: silence
1,0,2,5,9,3,5

10:25	9:35
10:35	8:50
10:00	8:35
9:35	8:55

Page 51, **Kitty Lit**
Riddle: cat-alogs
1,5,6-5,2,3,9,0

$15.65	$23.90
$10.45	$11.65
$3.50	$4.80

Page 56, **Buzzing Around**
Riddle: zom-bee
3,2,9-5,8,8

329	588
197	647
226	372
114	234

Page 47, **Cold Chills**
Riddle: scare it
1,2,3,0,6   4,5

12:30	6:45
11:45	6:05
10:05	5:10
9:15	4:35

Page 52, **In a Jam**
Riddle: traffic
1,3,2,5,5,8,0

$13.25	$5.80
$15.30	$15.35
$31.10	$22.50
$32.75	$25.60

Page 57, **Too Many Legs**
Riddle: bed
8,3,6

8	36
28	44
36	12
48	16

Page 48, **Simple Solution**
Riddle: holes
8,0,1,2,5

80	125
110	135
50	45
35	15

Page 53, **Day to Day**
Riddle: week
1,7,7,4

17	74
10	44
31	30

Page 58, **Drink-It!**
Riddle: croak
4 0,2,3,6

40	236
104	276
96	20
128	32

Page 49, **Hungry Birds**
Riddle: tweets
1,8,2,2,1,9

$1.82	$2.19
$1.87	$0.69
$1.25	$0.54

Page 54, **Treat of the Week**
Riddle: sundae
4,7,5,1,0,2

475	102
481	67
389	119
365	28